D0547259

This book is dedicated to the LAKOTA PEOPLE

and to all
NATIVE AMERICANS

# CONTENTS

Frank Fools Crow and Mathew King

© 1994 by Beyond Words Publishing, Inc., courtesy of Mathew King's family

# Noble Red Man

# Noble Red
# Man

## Lakota Wisdomkeeper Mathew King

Compiled and

edited by

## Harvey Arden

Co-author of *Wisdomkeepers*

BEYOND
WORDS
*Publishing*
I    N    C

*With special thanks to Lavon King*

BEYOND WORDS PUBLISHING INC.
20827 N.W. Cornell Road, Suite 500
Hillsboro, Oregon 97124-9808
503 •531 •8700
1 •800 •284 •9673

Text copyright © 1994 by Harvey Arden

Feather motif copyright © 1994 by Art Wolfe

All rights reserved. No part of this book may be reproduced or transmitted in any form or by any means, electronic or mechanical, including photocopying, recording, or by any information storage and retrieval system, without the written permission of Beyond Words Publishing, Inc., except where permitted by law.

Every effort has been made to locate the copyright owners of the photographs in this book.

The information contained in this book is intended to be educational and not for diagnosis, prescription, or treatment of any health disorder whatsoever. This information should not replace competent medical care. The editor and publisher are in no way liable for any use or misuse of the material.

DESIGN •Principia Graphica
ADVISORY CONSULTANT •Carl Heinze

Printed in the United States of America
Distributed to the book trade by
Publishers Group West

The Library of Congress has cataloged the hardcover edition as follows:

Noble Red Man : Lakota Wisdomkeeper : Mathew King /
    compiled and edited by Harvey Arden : co-author of Wisdomkeepers.
        p. cm.
        ISBN 1-885223-01-3 ISBN 1-58270-078-8 (pbk.)
        1. Noble Red Man.  2. Teton Indians—Biography.  3. Teton Indians—
Religion.  4. Teton Indians—Government relations.  5. Indians of
North America—Great Plains—Religion.  I. Arden, Harvey.
E99.T34N635  1994
973'.04975'0092—dc20
        (B)                                                                94-25672
                                                                              CIP

The corporate mission of
Beyond Words Publishing, Inc:
"Inspire to Integrity"

# EDITOR'S FOREWORD

MATHEW KING—Chief Noble Red Man—refuses to step aside in my memory. Of the scores of American Indian traditional Elders I have known over the years, he stands forth in my mind as the most luminous in spiritual insight and poetic power. His visionary message resonates in my soul, reverberates in my conscience.

As a longtime spokesman for the traditional chiefs of the Lakota (Sioux) Nation and official Interpreter for Frank Fools Crow, the famed Lakota high ceremonial chief, Mathew King was one of the preeminent leaders of the great Indian Reawakening that began in the late 1960s.

A tireless and fearless "spirit-warrior" on behalf of Indian causes, he gave political and spiritual counsel to the angry young activists of the American Indian Movement (AIM) during and after the historic 1973 "Occupation" of the little reservation community of Wounded Knee—an armed insurrection protesting long-standing abuses on the reservation. While hundreds of federal marshals and FBI agents besieged the militants in their fortified compound for seventy-one days, Mathew and Fools Crow quietly counseled the defenders within while negotiating with federal officials in finally ending the standoff. One of those officials, dismayed by Mathew's unyielding attitude, called him "the mean one of the bunch." But there was no meanness in Mathew King, only a fierce and implacable determination to see justice done for his people. "I'm an Indian warrior," he once told me with fire in his eyes. "I'll fight till they kill me!"

THE GREATEST CAUSE of his life was to see the Black Hills returned to the Lakota people. To Mathew, the Fort Laramie Treaty of 1868 was a sacred document, setting aside the Black Hills and adjacent lands "for the absolute and undisturbed use" of the Lakota people. Just five years after its ratification, an 1873 expedition led by General George Armstrong Custer discovered gold in "them thar hills," and within months the United States government, in flagrant violation of the Fort Laramie Treaty, encouraged thousands of gold prospectors to invade Lakota territory. This and other treaty violations soon led to open warfare between United States troops and the "hostiles"—among them Crazy Horse and Sitting Bull— culminating in Custer's defeat on the Little Big Horn in June 1876 and the subsequent crushing of Indian armed resistance. In 1877, Congress enacted a bill unilaterally expropriating the Black Hills—an act the U.S. Court of Claims, nearly a century later, would call "the most ripe and rank case of dishonorable dealing in our history." When the U.S. Supreme Court in 1980 awarded the Lakota people $106 million in monetary compensation for the acknowledged theft of the Black Hills, traditionalists like Mathew and Fools Crow rallied their people to reject the money, holding out for the return of at least part of the sacred hills themselves. The unpaid monies remain in the U.S. Treasury—totaling, as of this writing, nearly $400 million with accumulated interest.

I FIRST MET MATHEW in late February 1983. Writer-photographer Steve Wall and I had driven from Rapid City through South Dakota's bleakly beautiful Badlands to the Pine Ridge reservation to attend a ceremony on Wounded Knee Hill commemorating the tenth anniversary of the 1973 Occupation. On this site, in 1890, United States troops slaughtered hundreds of Chief Big Foot's band of defenseless men, women, and children in the infamous Wounded Knee Massacre—the final and perhaps the most shameless "battle" of the Indian wars. That both the Massacre and the Occupation took place on this forlorn hilltop has made the place doubly tragic, doubly holy.

We watched as ceremonial chief Frank Fools Crow raised his Sacred Pipe to the sky, pleading for a sign that the Creator still loved his Indian children. To our amazement, as the ceremony ended, a lone eagle—the eyes of the Creator in Indian belief—materialized out of that otherwise empty blue dome of South Dakota sky, circling high above our heads for fully ten minutes before finally disappearing. "Look! Up there!" someone shouted. "Now you know the power of Wounded Knee!"

The next day we drove out to the reservation hamlet of Kyle to speak with Mathew King, the official Interpreter for Fools Crow, who spoke little English. We knocked on the screen door of Mathew's small government-built house, its cracked and peeling walls painted a fading Pepto-Bismol pink. An elderly man came to the door, his face lit by a radiant smile.

"Come on in, you guys," he said in a warm, welcoming voice, leading us into the sparsely furnished living room. When we attempted to explain why we were there, Mathew waved his hand impatiently in the air, abruptly dismissing our explanations.

"I know why you're here!" he announced. "White Man came to this country and forgot his original Instructions. We Indians have never forgotten our Instructions. So you're here looking for the Instructions you lost. I can't tell you what those were, but maybe there are some things that I can explain . . . ."

TALKING WITH MATHEW was a powerful, at times overpowering, experience. Gentle, witty, even jovial on the surface, he could swing without the slightest hitch from casual laughter to the most exquisite philosophical contemplation, then launch without pause into a soul-singeing fire-and-brimstone sermon on the White Man's perfidies. His very words seemed to burn and smoke. Peering deep and hard into my eyes, he said, "You killed our people. You killed our chiefs. You stole our land." I knew he wasn't speaking of some abstract generic White Man. He was speaking about *me*!

And yet he was without hatred. He spoke not of revenge but of reconciliation. Despite the centuries-long Holocaust perpetrated against his people—a Holocaust he saw as ongoing—he put forth the astonishing message that the world is essentially good, that there is no evil in God, the Great Spirit, the Great Reality.

"Put goodness into the world!" he told me again and again. "That's the most important thing. That's your job as a human being!"

MATHEW defied stereotypes. "I'm no beads-and-feathers Indian or carnival chief," he once told me. "I'm the real thing." He was a major figure, along with Fools Crow, in the revival of the Sun Dance among Indian peoples around the country. "The most important thing I do is teach," he said, "and the most important thing I teach is the Sun Dance." In this central ritual of Plains Indian belief, voluntary participants are pierced with skewers through their chest muscles and must pull free from the Sacred Tree, or Sun Dance Pole, as they circle with eyes gazing into the sun.

Although a reviver of the long-banned Sun Dance and other sacred Lakota ceremonies, he spoke most often of "God" rather than "the Great Spirit"—a legacy, no doubt, of his partly Christian upbringing. Though he often referred to God as "He" and "Him," he would be the first to insist that God has no gender. "We have to use those kinds of words because you can't just say 'It,'" he explained. "God's never an 'It.'"

He spoke English not in the Victorian flourishes often ascribed to Indian chiefs in the past, but in a rough-hewn colloquial vernacular—disarmingly simple, yet capable of expressing the finest subtleties of thought and feeling and spirit. His visionary message speaks not only to his own people, but to all humankind.

MATHEW'S VISIONARY view of history may not agree
with historical accounts. The latter tell us that Siouan-
speaking peoples lived as sedentary agriculturists in
permanent earthen-lodge villages in the Carolinas before
being driven north and west after about 1600 by the
imperialist-minded Iroquois and encroaching whites; by
the early 1700s, they had drifted up the Mississippi
Valley to a new home territory in the deep woodlands of
what is now Minnesota. Hard-pressed by the local
Ojibway, who had only recently acquired guns from their
French patrons, some of these Siouan-speaking peoples
ventured west out of the woodlands onto the Great
Plains—by some accounts first reaching the Black Hills
in 1775. These became the so-called Western or Teton or
Lakota Sioux—the word *Sioux* being a French corruption
of an Ojibway word for "little snake," that is, "enemy."

Once out on the Plains, the Lakota gradually
acquired guns of their own, along with horses from the
Western tribes. Exchanging lodges for the more portable
tipis of the Plains peoples, and trading the "sedentary
agriculturist" life for a new existence based on buffalo
hunting, they literally reinvented themselves as a people
in the course of a generation or two. The classic era of
the archetypal horseback-riding, buffalo-hunting Sioux
warrior dashing across the Plains with his eagle-feather
bonnet fluttering in the wind had its beginnings no
earlier than about 1760, its heyday from about 1820 to
1860, and its abrupt and tragic finale no later than 1880,
little more than a century after it had begun.

When Mathew speaks of his people having lived in
the Black Hills for "millions" of years, he speaks not in a

historical but in a visionary sense. The white historians may be "right," but Mathew is also "right" in his own way.

MATHEW ESCHEWED the use of the word *Sioux*. "We are Lakota!" he would declare emphatically. In the complex and often confusing nomenclature on the subject, the Lakota or Teton or Western Sioux comprise the largest and best known of the three main divisions of the Great Sioux Nation—the others being the Nakota— also known as the Yankton or Central Sioux—and the Dakota—also known as the Santee or Eastern Sioux.

To complicate matters further, the Lakota themselves are subdivided into seven tribes, or nations. Mathew belonged to the Oglala, now centered at Pine Ridge. Oglala chieftains Red Cloud and Crazy Horse inflicted two of the worst defeats suffered by United States government forces during the Indian wars. Red Cloud routed the bluecoats at the Fetterman "Massacre" of 1866 and harassed government outposts and trails during the so-called "Red Cloud's War" of 1866–68, forcing the government to abandon several forts and trails. Crazy Horse (who was Mathew's great-uncle), along with the Hunkpapa Lakota holy man Sitting Bull, led Sioux forces in the destruction of Custer's Seventh Cavalry on the Little Big Horn on June 25, 1876. Little more than a year later, Crazy Horse was dead, murdered through treachery. Within a few years, the proud Sitting Bull was touring in Buffalo Bill's Wild West extravaganza. (He, too, would be murdered in 1890, just before the Wounded Knee Massacre.) The glory years were over, and the reservation period—into which Mathew King was born—had begun.

TAPES AND NOTES from our conversations with Mathew formed the basis for a chapter in a book Steve Wall and I co-authored in 1990—*Wisdomkeepers: Meetings with Native American Spiritual Elders* (Beyond Words Publishing, Inc.).

Mathew never saw that book. He passed on to what he called "the Great Reality" in March 1989, at age eighty-seven. He often spoke to me of plans to write a book of his own, but he never found the time in a busy and tumultuous life devoted to his people. I was glad, at least, to have had a part in bringing a few precious fragments of his visionary message to the reading public. Yet something still nagged at me.

During one of our conversations, Mathew had told me: "You're on a spirit-journey. God's making use of you. He's sending you out to reveal the life of the Indian people. You should be grateful He's found a use for you."

But were my "spirit-journey" and my obligation to Mathew over now that *Wisdomkeepers* had been published?

On an impulse last year, having just completed another project, I dug the old tapes and notes of Mathew's words out of a dusty file. In some inexplicable way they seemed to be calling out to me. I listened to the tapes again and again, transcribed them word for word, reviewed the thick sheaf of notes, and concluded that *Wisdomkeepers* was, indeed, just the beginning. There was so much more here, truly wonderful thoughts and visions and memories—a whole interlocking spiritual philosophy, a kind of Native American testament or gospel. There wasn't quite enough for even a small book, perhaps, yet enough to set me thinking that the book

Mathew had envisioned might still be put together with some additional materials. I remembered Mathew mentioning some tapes and notes he'd made for use in the book he'd hoped to write.

Perhaps they still existed?

On the chance that they did, I drove out to Pine Ridge to talk with Mathew's daughter Lavon. I knocked on the screen door of the same little government-built house I had visited in 1983. I could almost sense Mat standing there as he had done that day ten years earlier— a spry man of about eighty, of medium height and slightly stocky, with close-cut white hair and that radiant smile on his face.

His daughter Lavon came to the door. I could see Mathew's face in hers. When I explained to her that I hoped to edit her father's words into a book and that I'd come out to Pine Ridge looking for more materials, Lavon literally clapped her hands with joy. She pointed to a small red trunk sitting on the floor in a corner of the living room—the same room where Mat and I had had many of our conversations.

"The stuff you're looking for is right there in that trunk," she said. "My dad left them—a bunch of notes and old reel-to-reel tapes of him telling his stories and visions. Before he died, he told me to save them—that there'd come a time when they'd be important. Now I know why."

I DROVE to the nearby Black Hills the next day and climbed Bear Butte, holy mountain of the Lakota people, where Mathew so often went to "talk to God." I did my best to commune with Him. No vision came to me, I confess—but I walked back down with an unshakable determination to see Mathew's book to completion.

Mathew's presence has filled my little basement study these past months as I've assembled his words from my own materials and Lavon's and edited them into the form you find in these pages.

Yes, Mathew, your book is complete at last.

This, then, as I hope he'd have wanted to see it, is the visionary message of Mathew King—Chief Noble Red Man.

Harvey Arden
*October 1994*

# NOBLE RED MAN

Mathew King—Chief Noble Red Man

© 1994  by Chris Spotted Eagle

# WHO I AM

I'm an Indian. I'm one of God's children.

It's time Indians tell the world what we know . . . about Nature and about God. So I'm going to tell what I know and who I am. You better listen. You've got a lot to learn.

I'm a full-blood Indian from the Pine Ridge reservation in South Dakota. My Indian name is Noble Red Man. That was my grandfather's name. White Man mistranslated his name as "King," so they call me Mathew King. But my real name, my Lakota name, is Noble Red Man.

I speak for the Lakota people. You call us "Sioux." But that's White Man's name for us.
Our real name is "Lakota." That means "People together," or "Allies."
That's what we call ourselves.
And that's what God calls us.

Call me a chief of the Lakota. I'm a speaker for the chiefs. I say what I have to say. That's my duty. If I don't say it, who's going to say it for me?

I'm a prophet of the Indian people. I can see what's coming. I prophesy what's going to happen. I walk with the Great Spirit, with God. Wakan-Tanka, that's what we call him in Lakota. I talk to Him. The Great Spirit guides me in my life.

Sometimes He comes to me and tells me what to say. Other times I just speak for myself, for Mathew King.

❖

# THE GREAT MYSTERIOUS

You can call Wakan-Tanka by any name you like. In English I call Him God or the Great Spirit.

He's the Great Mystery, the Great Mysterious. That's what Wakan-Tanka really means—the Great Mysterious.

You can't define Him. He's not actually a "He" or a "She," a "Him" or a "Her." We have to use those kinds of words because you can't just say "It." God's never an "It."

So call Wakan-Tanka whatever you like.

Just be sure to call Him.

He wants to talk to you.

✤

# TALKING TO GOD

When we want wisdom we go up on the hill and talk to God. Four days and four nights, without food and water. Yes, you can talk to God up on a hill by yourself. You can say anything you want. Nobody's there to listen to you. That's between you and God and nobody else.

It's a great feeling to be talking to God. I know. I did it way up on the mountain. The wind was blowing. It was dark. It was cold. And I stood there and I talked to God.

✤

# LISTENING TO GOD

When I go up on the hill to pray I don't just talk to God. I try to get the talking over quick. Mostly I'm listening.

Listening to God—that's praying, too.

You've got to listen. God's talking to you right now. He's telling you all the words you've got to speak and all the things you've got to do in this life. If you don't listen, you don't hear what God's saying, and then you don't know what God wants you to say and do.

So that's how you pray to God.

You *listen*.

✤

# PRAYER

I pray, pray, and pray before I go to bed. Every time I wake in the middle of the night I pray to God. I thank Him for the life He gives me. I ask Him for understanding. During the day there's things I have to do. People come to me, they ask me to go out and talk. I do it when I can. Otherwise I like to stay home and study, pray, and clean my Peace Pipe.

Maybe some think I should be doing something else. But God knows I'm doing the right thing.

There's only one time to pray, and that's now. There's no better time to pray than now. Now is the only time you need to pray. You can't pray any other time than right now!

# Visions, Dreams, and Miracles

We live by visions. We live by dreams. We live by miracles. Miracles come to us in our everyday lives, in our ceremonies, in our prayers.

Every day is a miracle to us.

Many times I've seen the eagle come out of the empty sky and circle over our heads when we blow the eagle-bone whistle. The eagle is the witness of the Great Spirit, the eyes of God.

Once I had an eagle dream. I left my bed and flew with the eagle out below the sun and above the clouds. After we circled around up there ten times, I flew back down to my bed. The eagle came down with me and flew around my head four times, then flew away.

Now, whenever the eagle joins us in our ceremony, I always say a friendly hello to him.

He remembers me, and I remember him.

We keep an eye out for each other.

The eagle's my symbol. In our Way, you always have a symbol. That's your power. It reminds you of God. It reminds you to do good.

Some missionaries came to one of our ceremonies. They watched us while we danced. I told them, "Everybody, look up in the sky. See, the eagle's come to join us!"

The eagle came over and flew right down into our ceremony. He stood there on one foot, with one leg up in the air. He carried two feathers in his claw and he put them on his head like a crown. Then he started dancing. We danced with him.

We all cried to see the eagle dance. Even the missionaries cried. "We can't believe it!" they said. "It can't be happening!"

But it happened.

God danced with us!

I've seen the spirits of our ancestors come join us when we sing the spirit-songs. They sing with us all night. They take our hands and dance with us until they fade away with the morning.

I've sat down with the buffalo and they don't bother me. They know I'm an Indian. They nurse their calves beside me and let me be. Any white man try that and the only miracle'd be if he got out of there alive.

I've gone up on the mountain praying for a vision and talked to Crazy Horse. I've talked to Red Cloud and Noble Red Man. They teach me things the living have forgot, things the White Man can never know or understand.

❖

# GOD'S INSTRUCTIONS

White Man came to this country and forgot his original Instructions. We Indians have never forgotten our Instructions.

God gives His Instructions to every creature, according to His plan for the world. He gave His Instructions to all the things of Nature. The pine tree and the birch tree, they still follow their Instructions and do their duty in God's world. The flowers, even the littlest flower, they bloom and they pass away according to His Instructions. The birds, even the smallest bird, they live and they fly and they sing according to His Instructions.

Should human beings be any different?

❖

# RESPECT

Our Instructions are very simple—to respect the Earth and each other, to respect *life itself*. That's our first Commandment, the first line of our Gospel.

Respect is our Law—respect for God's Creation, for all the living beings of this Earth, for our mother the Earth herself.

We can't harm the Earth or the water because we respect their place in the world. We could never kill all the buffalo because that shows no respect for why the buffalo are here.

You need to respect the animal you kill. It's following God's Instructions.

*© 1994 by Harvey Arden*

You must respect other people's dreams. Respect their dreams and they'll respect your dreams.

We need to have respect even for those not yet born, for the generations to come. They have their rights, too. We must respect them.

That is our religion and our Law. That is our Way. Those are our Instructions.

We Indians haven't forgotten them and we never will.

❖

# GOODNESS

Goodness is the natural state of this world. The world is good! Even when it seems evil, it's good. There's only goodness in God. And that same goodness is in us all. You can feel it in yourself. You know when you feel good inside.

Yes, you're God's child, too. You are good. You are sacred. Respect yourself. Love the goodness in yourself.

Then, put that goodness into the world.

That's everybody's Instructions.

God made you so you feel good when you do right. Watch when you feel good and follow that good feeling. The good feeling comes from God. When you feel good, God feels good, too. God and you feel good together.

❖

# EVERYONE IS SACRED

Everyone is sacred. You're sacred and I'm sacred. Every time you blink your eye, or I blink my eye, God blinks His eye. God sees through your eyes and my eyes.

We are sacred.

❖

# God's Mercy

God shows His mercy every day. Whether you're wrong or whether you're right, He still loves you. He loves what He has created.

❖

# Sharing

We Lakota people have our giveaways. When something important happens we celebrate by sharing what we have. There's nothing we like more than to give gifts to others, to share with others. Even the poorest of us share what we have. We are a sharing people.

The more you share the more you're given to share. God gives you more of his goodness to share with others. When you share with others you share with God.

God loves a sharer.

❖

# GOD MADE EVERYTHING
# SO SIMPLE

God made everything so simple. Our lives are very simple. We do what we please. The only law we obey is the natural Law, God's Law. We abide only by that.

We don't need your church. We have the Black Hills for our church. And we don't need your Bible. We have the wind and the rain and the stars for our Bible. The world is an open Bible for us. We've studied it for millions of years.

We've learned that God rules the Universe and that everything God made is living. Even the rocks are alive. When we use them in our sweat ceremony we talk to them . . . and they talk back to us.

❖

# GOD'S TABERNACLE

The Universe is the tabernacle of God.

When the wind blows, that's the breath of God.

When you or I breathe, that's also the breath of God.


God gave us peace. Go up on a hill early tomorrow morning and look out into the valley. See how peaceful it is. Everything's quiet. All you hear is birds singing, praising God.

❖

# WHITE MAN GETS EVERYTHING WRONG

White Man gets everything wrong. He says we're warlike when we're peaceful. See, he calls this headdress a war bonnet. Sure, we used it in war, but most of the time it was for ceremony, not war. Each feather stands for a good deed. See, I have thirty-six in mine. It's not about war. It's about who we are.

When we sing songs the White Man calls them war songs. But they're not war songs, they're prayers to God. We have drums, so White Man calls them war drums. But they're not for war, they're for talking to God. There's no such thing as a war drum.

White Man sees how our warriors paint their faces, so he calls it war paint. But it's not for war, it's to make it so God can see our faces clearly if we have to die.

White Man says our Lakota people came to the Black Hills only a couple of centuries ago. He's wrong. We've been here millions of years. White Man says God made the world in seven days. He's wrong there, too. God's been making the world for millions of years, and He's still not finished.

He makes it new each morning when the sun comes up. If he didn't—*poof!*—the world would be gone. That's why we send up our prayers to Him each morning and each evening—to thank Him for the world.

If we didn't thank Him, He might not keep making the world new. It would all be gone.

And what would White Man have to steal from us then?

❖

Mathew King and Frank Fools Crow
in their ceremonial eagle-feather headdresses

© 1994 by Beyond Words Publishing, Inc., courtesy of Mathew King's family

# HOW I KNOW
# WHAT I KNOW

People ask me how I know what I know.

I tell them, I listened to the old people, the Elders. They pass on the stories that have been handed down through the generations. When I was a boy I always sat down with the Grandfathers and the Grandmothers, and I listened.

They told wonderful stories. They never lied.

Maybe those stories would seem fantastic to an outsider, but they were true.

From the Elders I learned about the spirit-warriors who control the air and the Universe.

They gave me the names for all the stars, the Morning Star and the Evening Star, the Big Dipper and all that.

They brought the stars to life.

Is there any power greater than that?

❖

# THE WAY OF THE ELDERS

We follow the teachings of the Elders and our ancestors. In our Way, the Elders give spiritual direction to the people. The wisdom of thousands of years flows through their lips.

In our Way, when we grow old we become Elders.

In White Man's way, when you grow old you just grow old.

# THE FAMILY

To us the family is very important. The whole family is responsible for the children. Not only the mother and father but all the family, the grandmothers and the grandfathers, the aunts and uncles, the sisters and brothers, they all teach the children. They all watch out for each other.

It saddens me when I see the government building old-age homes for our Elders. That's White Man's way. The Elders belong at the center of the family, not off by themselves, left to die.

Without them it's not a family anymore.

Without the family you're nobody, just a seed in the wind without a garden to grow in. The family is our garden. It's a garden of souls.

❖

# DEATH SONG

I feel sorry for the White Man. He's got no death song. He's got to die in silence or die screaming, but he's got no song to sing. I have my song. It was my grandfather's song and his grandfather's before him. It's a million years old. We died to that song before the White Man ever came here.

Lots of our own people don't have a song anymore. They lost or forgot them. They don't know how to die. Many times I've taught my song to chiefs who don't know theirs.

I know how to die.

A man needs a song or he dies like a dog.

❖

# THE YEARS OF OUR LIVES

Once people lived for 900 years or more. Your Bible says that, and I believe it on that point. That was in the beginning of time when God taught the human race His power. Human beings obeyed that power and lived a long and useful life. But then people went against His Law and He cut down their number of years. It went from 800 to 600 to 400 to 200 years, and so on.

We Indians remember when some of our people lived to be 140. That was about ninety years ago. Today our expected life span on the reservation is barely forty.

Pretty soon we will be born in the morning and die in the evening.

# The Three Powers
# of the World

God put Three Powers into the world for us to use. We need them all. We Indians know all three. It took us a million years to find them.

There's the material power, the spiritual power, and the supernatural power. The material power is the goodness of this Earth. The spiritual power is the goodness of human beings. The supernatural power is the goodness of God, the Great Spirit.

The Three Powers are all separate. They're not connected.

It's the job of human beings to make that connection.

We connect the Three Powers with our prayers, with our ceremonies, with our deeds. Every good deed is a pillar of the Creation. Every prayer holds up the world. Our ceremony, our Sun Dance, keeps the Universe in harmony by connecting the Three Powers.

Material power has the strongest hold on people. It's the power God gave us to use and enjoy the things of this Earth.

Some people think it's the only power. They're like the ones who take the uranium out of the ground where God put it and build an atomic bomb to kill human beings. Then they go to their church and call out, "God bless us! Help us rule your world!"

Impossible! God's not helping them. They can't rule this world. This world is God's, and only God rules the world.

The second power is the spiritual power. Without the spiritual power the material power will destroy all life. Materialism without spirituality is the curse of this world.

Spiritual power is the power to do good. It's the power to pray, to talk to God, to listen to Him, to follow His Instructions. We don't have to do it. It's up to us.

That's the spiritual power, the second power God gave us.

It's what makes us human.

The third power is the supernatural power, the direct power of God entering into the world He made. It refers to God Himself, the Great Mysterious.

You can't use it for yourself. That's sorcery. It's supposed to use you.

Sometimes the supernatural power comes to help us. We can't control that power, but still it comes to help us when we need it. If you're open to God, if you're using your spiritual power, then God will use His supernatural power to help you.

It's the power that gives us eternal life.

It's the power that answers our prayers.

It's the Great Reality.

❖

# THE GREAT REALITY

Sometimes I see beyond this world. I see a Great Reality. It's the Great Reality of God.

You can't really describe it. There's no evil there. It's all good. There's no evil in God.

This world we live in comes out of that world like a drop of dew comes out of the morning sky, and we human beings come from that world and go back to it, just like the dewdrop.

It's where our prayers go.

There's buffalo there and spirit-warriors on their horses.

There's no suffering there.

It's the Great Reality, that's what I call it.

❖

# WOUNDED KNEE

When we occupied Wounded Knee in 1973 it was a matter of survival. We picked up the gun because it's our duty to survive as a people. That's God's Instructions to us. We must survive. We had to let the world know how our people are being destroyed. The U.S. government can't hide what they've done to us. The world had to know.

Now they know.

It's our duty to become a free people again,

to become part of the world of nations. We are a nation by every standard set by the United Nations. We have our own language, our own religion, our own land, our own history, our own culture going back to the beginning of time.

That's more than your U.S. government can say. You borrowed your language and your religion from someone else; you didn't create them. And you took your land from someone else, too. From us!

We Indians are a beautiful people, a peaceful people. Each and every one of us is a natural-born leader. We have so much to teach the world, so much to give other nations of people. We want our rightful place. You can't hide us from the world!

We had to stop the murders of our people, so in 1973 we took back a tiny piece of our own land, right there on the Pine Ridge reservation, the holy hill of Wounded Knee. That's where they slaughtered Big Foot and his band in 1890. Big Foot's people did nothing wrong. It was the dead of winter. They were coming down from North Dakota to find refuge here at Pine Ridge with Red Cloud. They were freezing. They were starving. They just wanted to survive. They were following God's Instructions.

They made camp at Wounded Knee. The soldiers came with guns. They surrounded Big Foot and his people like criminals. It was mostly old men, women, little children. Big Foot didn't want to fight. He was already sick with pneumonia. He was peaceful.

The soldiers lined them up in the cold and started taking away all their weapons. The third to the last man in line was treated very roughly by one of the soldiers, so he took out his gun and blew the soldier's brains out. The ones who escaped told our people all about it.

Then the soldiers on top of the hill started shooting, shooting everybody. Our people dropped down on the ground and the soldiers mowed down dozens of their own men. Our warriors tried to defend their people. They fought like hell but there was no chance. The soldiers slaughtered them, then slaughtered the elders and women and children.

Who ever heard of punishing the whole

family, the whole people for the misdeeds of one man? Is that your justice? Is that what your Constitution says? That's not God's Law.

Three hundred of us they slaughtered.

Our blood made Wounded Knee holy.

That's why we chose Wounded Knee for our Occupation. We didn't want to shoot anybody. Sure, we had our guns, but we didn't want to use them. The FBI surrounded us. I was there with the other Elders. We were the Peacemakers. Our warriors came to me and asked me what to do.

"Use the Pipe, the Sacred Pipe," I told them. "That's more powerful than any guns, more powerful even than an atom bomb!"

Seventy-one days we held them off. It wasn't guns that did that for us. It was the power of the Sacred Pipe, God's supernatural power.

So we avoided another massacre. Some got hurt, a few got killed, but we followed God's Instructions. We survived.

After that, many of our warriors were arrested and thrown in jail. Leonard Peltier and the others. Trumped-up charges. They don't care which one of us they get. Just get an

Indian. Get the first Indian you see. That's White Man's justice.

But we survived and we'll keep on surviving. That's what Wounded Knee is all about. Survival.

❖

# THE POWER
# OF NAMES

In our Way, names are important. Names have power.

I was given many names. Each explains a part of me. Every name has a history behind it. You give children special names to strengthen them in their lives. On a child's naming day we have a ceremony and a big giveaway. The family gives away all kinds of gifts, expensive things like beaded leggings and moccasins.

My grandmother did wonderful beadwork. Her gifts were treasures. At my naming ceremony, when I was a little boy, she gave me one of my names in honor of her husband, Chief Fast Thunder. He was a medicine man, a great chief who helped everybody, so she called me "Helper" in his honor. I've tried to live up to that name all my life.

Fast Thunder himself gave me another name that same day. He told how the Pawnees once ambushed one of our hunting parties. There were thirty-eight of our warriors and the Pawnees killed all but three. Three escaped. One of those was Fast Thunder. He said:

> I was hit with two arrows. One went clear through my body and stuck out my back. I broke off the head and pulled the shaft back out. The other arrow was just partly in my body, and I pulled that out, too. I hid in a gully in some tall grass and used my medicine herbs to treat my wounds.
> When the Pawnees left I crawled out and sang songs of grief as I walked among my dead comrades. They were scalped and mutilated, ears and fingers cut off, whole hands cut off. Later we would get our revenge. I got back to camp and my people nursed me back to health. I'm hard to kill!

So he gave me the name "Hard to Kill," and that's helped keep me alive all these years.

I'm proud to bear Noble Red Man's name. White Man didn't understand when they called him "King." We don't have kings. We don't have rulers. God made us a democracy. In our form of government everybody has a chance to talk. And the chiefs listen. They're not dictators.

White Man thinks he invented democracy, but God invented democracy!

Noble Red Man was a spiritual leader, a man of peace. He lived up near Pierre, on the Bad River. One day many years before I was born, some soldiers came and shot him. We're told Custer's nephew did that. He said, "I'm going to kill the first Indian I see." My grandfather Noble Red Man was the one. So he died for being an Indian.

Now I've got his name. I'm proud of that.

They gave me another name in honor of my grandfather Crazy Horse. You'd call him my granduncle, but to our people granduncles are grandfathers.

Crazy Horse was the greatest warrior. The

White Man never tamed him. He whipped Custer and his bluecoats at Little Big Horn. They say he killed 570 enemies with his own hands. He used to pray and fast in the wilderness. The Great Spirit was with him. He had special powers. Before a battle he rubbed a sacred stone all over himself and sprinkled dirt from a gopher hole over his body. This made all weapons powerless against him. When they shot him at close range they'd miss him. He had God's supernatural power. They couldn't hit him with their bullets.

Many times he went out on the warpath all by himself and he'd kill the enemy alone.

So, in his honor, they named me "Kills Enemy Alone." I've got that power, too, but I don't use it.

❖

Pipe ceremony at Little Big Horn on June 25, 1976

© 1994 by Beyond Words Publishing, Inc., courtesy of Mathew King's family

# A SAD STORY

It's a sad story about Fast Thunder and Crazy Horse. Both were my grandfathers. They fought together against other tribes and the U.S. soldiers. Both loved freedom, but Fast Thunder saw that the Indian didn't have a chance. He said, "White men are numerous as the grass that grows on the prairie. We can't keep fighting them. We have to work with them." Finally, he agreed to live on the reservation. He became a scout for the Army.

Crazy Horse went his own way. He wouldn't give in to the White Man. "Kill me if you want," he said, "but at least I'll die free!" He refused to live on the reservation.

Then the government sent Fast Thunder and some others to bring Crazy Horse back to Fort Robinson. They told him Crazy Horse would be safe—they just wanted to have a peace talk with him. Finally Fast Thunder helped talk him into it, and they brought Crazy Horse back to the fort. Crazy Horse figured it was a trick, but he knew his time had come. "My people have lost their freedom anyway," they heard him say, "so how can I be free all by myself?" He was ready to die. He had his death song ready, and he must have been singing it inside his head when they entered through the gate at Fort Robinson.

Fast Thunder thought he was doing a good thing. He thought he was saving Crazy Horse. But when they got inside the fort, the soldiers grabbed Crazy Horse. They started to put him in jail, but he went for his knife—the only weapon he had. A soldier speared him from behind with his bayonet, right through the kidney. Crazy Horse died—but he died free.

Crazy Horse used to say, "When I die I'll come back as thunder and lightning." So whenever it thunders and lightnings, we still hear him. Sometimes when I go up on Bear Butte, our holy mountain in the Black Hills, he speaks to me from the sky; his voice is thunder, his tongue is lightning.

My grandfather Fast Thunder was never the same after the soldiers fooled him and killed Crazy Horse. That was in 1877. He lived until 1914, but he was never the same. I got to know him when I was little. He was a good man, a great man who helped everybody. He became rich raising cattle. He had 707 spotted ponies, so they gave him the "707" brand. But all most people remembered about him was that he helped do in Crazy Horse. They never let him forget it. People had no mercy on him. Even today they haven't forgiven him.

Sometimes as a boy I'd go out walking with him in the hills, and he'd sit down by the creek and shake his head over and over.

"They tricked me," he'd say again and again. "They tricked me! They tricked me!"

I never saw anyone so sad.

❖

# WICKEDNESS

When I get mad I'm no good. I remember
how I used to get mad thinking about how they
murdered Noble Red Man and those other great
leaders—Crazy Horse, Sitting Bull, Big Foot,
and all the others. I was a young man, hot-
headed. My anger got the best of me. I couldn't
think right. I said, "I'm going to get back at
them every way I can." And I did. You'd
probably do the same thing.

I won't tell you what I did. There's a lot of
things I'm not telling. They're mine. We
revenge ourselves in many ways. But that only
makes us wicked, too.

My wife finally came to me. She said,
"Don't do that anymore. You're going to get
killed. And besides, it's *wrong*."

So I stopped. I tried peace instead.

Peace is harder, but it's the better way.

Peace is God's way.


One of the other names they gave me is "Big Leggings." I got that name from another of my grandfathers. I don't know why, but he always liked to wear big leggings. He was a warrior, feared by everyone. Some said he was a wicked man because he believed in violence. He'd go into an enemy's tent and he'd cut him up bad, take his scalp, and mutilate his other parts. He was a wicked man and they gave me his name. So maybe that's where I get my wicked streak. I've always got to watch out for that.

Wickedness lays heavy on the soul.

If you want to fly with the eagle, you can't be wicked.

# CHIEF SPOTTED TAIL
# ON WHITE MAN'S RELIGION

Here's what one of my grandfathers, Chief Spotted Tail, had to say a century ago about White Man's religion:

> I am bothered about what to believe. Some years ago a good man, as I think, came to see us. He talked me out of my old faith. And after a while, thinking he must know more about these matters than an ignorant Indian, I joined his church and became a Methodist. After a while he went away. Another man came and taught and I became a Baptist. Then another came and taught and I became a Presbyterian. Now another one has come and wants me to be an Episcopalian.

Chief Spotted Tail went on:

All these people tell different stories and each wants me to believe that his special way is the only way to be good and save my soul. I have about made up my mind that either they all lie or that they don't know any more about it than I did at first. I have always believed in the Great Spirit and worshipped Him in my own way. These people don't seem to want to change my belief in the Great Spirit, but to change my way of talking to Him.

White Men have education and books and ought to know exactly what to do. But hardly any two of them agree on what should be done.

❖

# SITTING BULL'S DEFENSE

And here's what another of our great chiefs, Sitting Bull, had to say in defense of his character:

> What treaty that the whites have kept has the red man broken? Not one!
>
> What treaty that the whites ever made with us red men have they kept? Not one!
>
> When I was a boy the Sioux owned the world. The sun rose and set on our lands. We sent ten thousand horsemen into battle. Where are the warriors today? Who slew them? Where are our lands? Who owns them?
>
> What white man can say I ever stole his land or a penny of his money? Yet they say I am a thief.

Chief Sitting Bull went on:

What white woman, however lonely, was ever, when a captive, insulted by me? Yet they say I am a bad Indian.

What white man has ever seen me drunk? Who has ever come to me hungry and gone unfed? Who has ever seen me beat my wives or abuse my children? What law have I broken?

Is it wrong for me to love my own?

Is it wicked of me because my skin is red? Because I am a Sioux? Because I was born where my fathers lived? Because I would die for my people and my country?

# THE BLACK HILLS

The Black Hills are where we came out of the Earth, where our ancestors are buried, where we go for sacred ceremony. They are the birthplace of the Lakota people.

The White Man wants us to take a hundred million dollars for our Black Hills. But a hundred billion wouldn't be enough. Not even four hundred billion! That wouldn't even pay for the damages you've done.

You can never pay us for what you've stolen and destroyed. You can never pay for all the eagles you've killed, for all the buffalo, all the wild game. No, and you can never pay us for all the Indians you've killed . . . .

The Black Hills aren't for sale.

What if we offered you a hundred million dollars for the Vatican, for Jerusalem?

❖

# HOW WILL YOU
# PAY US?

White Man thinks he can buy everything.
He thinks money can buy our Black Hills. He's
wrong again. God gave us those hills. They're
holy. You can't have them!

You think it's an accident that the White
Man drove us back into these hills and badlands
only to find that this land was rich with gold
and copper and coal and uranium? Now you
want the uranium. But you can't have it. We are
the guardians of the uranium of Grandmother
Earth. You can't have it. You'll only use it to
destroy God's world.

I asked one of your congressmen where the
United States was going to get all the money
that your own Supreme Court says you owe us
for stealing the Black Hills. He said, "Why,
we'll get it from the U.S. Treasury."

I had to laugh. I told him, "And where did
your Treasury get that money? I'll tell you
where you got it. You stole it from *us*. That's
not your money. That's Indian money. You stole

our hills, our resources, then you put the profits in your Treasury. And now you're going to take a little bit of that money, the money you stole, and give it back to us as full payment.

"You're going to pay us with our own money!

"You must think we're crazy, but we're not.

"We want our hills back!"

❖

# YOU HAVE NEVER THANKED US

You White Men have taken everything and given us nothing, but worst of all, you have never thanked us!

You've got to change your ways. I don't have to change. You're the ones who have to change. I live by God's power and I do what He wants me to do.

We Indians lived a good life, a happy life, until you came here and made it miserable. Who gave you the right to do that? You killed our people. You stole our land. But God gave us this land. You can't take it away!

❖

# GOD'S JUDGMENT: A PROPHECY

I prophesy many things that come to pass. God is going to put a judgment on the world. He's mad. I'm sorry it's going to happen. He's not going to destroy the whole world, but every living thing will perish, and it'll be maybe another million years before a new life begins again. All because of White Man's wickedness.

Grandmother Earth will be alone. She's going to rest.

You're going to fall and fall hard. You're going to be crying and wailing. You'll realize you can't get away with destroying God's world.

Don't think you can get away with it.

God's going to wipe the wickedness from the Earth. You can see His signs. Out on the West Coast, Mount St. Helens volcano—that's a sign. And there's going to be earthquakes. Maybe half of California and half of Washington and Oregon will go into the water. The same in the East and in the South.

You're going to have volcanoes and earthquakes and hurricanes. It's God giving signs to the White Man, punishing him for not paying his debt to the Indian people, for destroying the land with his greed. And it will get worse until you pay us what you owe us, what you promised us . . . until you give us what is ours.

You white people are going to learn the most important lesson—that God is the most important thing there is.

We Indians aren't afraid to die. We've got a place to go, a better place, so we don't care. We're ready. We just want you white people to know. Maybe you can change, maybe you can stop what's coming. There's not much time.

It's going to happen. Take it from me. Tell them I, Noble Red Man, said so!

❖

INDIANS PRAYING
DO NOT PASS BEYOND
THIS POINT

A sign alerts visitors to Bear Butte State Park

© 1994 by Harvey Arden

# A Vision

Once when I was up on the mountain, I prayed to God to give us a cure for diabetes. And while I was there, somebody said, "Turn around!" So I turned around and there was the most beautiful Indian woman I had ever seen.

She had long black hair and a wonderful face. She held something out to me in her hand. It was those little dark berries you find on a certain tree. She held them out, but before I could reach out my hand she disappeared.

I know who she was. She's the one who brought the Sacred Pipe to our people. We call her White Buffalo Calf Woman. God sent her to save the Indian people.

That was long ago. At that time we were starving. The children were crying. Women with babies could give no milk because they had nothing to eat. Our hunters circled far and wide to hunt the buffalo and wild game, but there was nothing, not even a rabbit, not even a bird. We were being punished for having strayed from God, for not knowing Him. His wrath was on us.

But still God loved us. He wanted to give His Indian children the Pipe so we could talk and pray with Him whenever we wanted. So God sent that beautiful White Buffalo Calf Woman to us with the Pipe. She took the bundle with the Pipe on her back and set off to carry it to the Indian people. But on her way she met two warriors. She set her bundle down and looked at them. They saw how beautiful she was. Man, you can't resist a woman like that! No man is strong enough to resist a woman. You just can't do it.

Well, the first warrior was so afraid when he saw her that he just fell down, too scared to move. But the other warrior right away had evil thoughts about that woman because she was so pretty. So she called the one with the wicked mind over to her and a cloud engulfed him, and when the cloud went away he just lay there, skin and bones, dead, with worms crawling all over him.

After that, White Buffalo Calf Woman went with the good warrior to where a group of our Lakota people were camping. She called the people together into a ceremony and she presented us with the Sacred Pipe.

"You've strayed from God," she said. "He can't hear your prayers. That's why things have been going wrong for you. So from now on, whenever you pray in your ceremony, use this holy Pipe that I'm giving to you today. It will give you wisdom, courage, and strength. When you use it the Great Spirit will hear your prayers and answer them."

As she left the camp a cloud engulfed her and a white buffalo calf came out of the cloud and ran away into the hills and up into the sky.

To this day we keep and honor that holy Pipe.

When we pray with it, White Buffalo Calf Woman guides the tobacco smoke and our prayers up to the Great Spirit.

He hears us and blesses His Indian children.

So I knew when I saw her up on the mountain in my vision that this was the same woman. But she disappeared before I could take those berries from her hand.

Later on, when I got diabetes, I forgot about the berries. They sent me to White Man's doctors. They gave me pills. Every morning I had to take insulin. I spent a lot of time in the hospital.

Then I remembered White Buffalo Calf Woman and those little berries. I picked some, boiled them, strained the juice, and drank it. It's so bitter it took the sugar right out of my body. The doctors checked me and were amazed. They said the diabetes was gone. I didn't have to take insulin anymore. They asked me how I did it, but I didn't say.

God gave us medicine to share with people, but if the White Man gets his hands on it he'll charge you a great price and will let you die if you don't have the money. God's medicine is free. God doesn't charge a fee. We don't give money to God. We give Him our prayers, our thanks. And sometimes we give Him the only thing that's really ours. Our flesh. Our pain. That's what the Sun Dance is all about—giving God our flesh, our pain, and—never forget—a prayer of thanks.

❖

# THE POWER
# OF THE PIPE

The Peace Pipe is our greatest weapon. It's our holy power. It's God's power. The Pipe mediates between human beings and God.

To receive the Pipe, to receive God's gift, you've got to be pure in your heart, mind, body, and soul. And never forget that, after the prayers are over, you've got to live that life—a life with God. That's the hardest part.

❖

# GOD'S MEDICINE

People ask me if I'm a medicine man. Well, I'm not. Some of our Indian people were blessed with that power in the past. They're all gone now.

Today our people know only a little medicine. It's a special knowledge. You can't read it in books. You can't inherit it. It can't be bought or sold. This knowledge can come to you only through the Great Spirit.

We had great medicine men only fifty or sixty years ago. I'll tell you about one I knew when I was a boy. This was in 1908 or 1910, and my family was traveling from Pine Ridge to a summer get-together in Santee, Nebraska. There were no cars in those days. We traveled in covered wagons, and it took twelve days to get to Santee. On the way it was so hot my little sister—she was about five—got sick. Sunstroke or something. By the time we reached Santee she was unconscious, almost dead. We set up a tipi and put her in there, out of the sun.

My mother saw our cousin Vine Deloria, and he took one look at my sister and said, "Let's go get Dr. Queen—he's here!"

So they ran and brought a man back to the tipi. He wore a suit and a necktie, not Indian dress. But he had black hair flowing down to his waist. He was a medicine man—one of the greatest.

He put his hand on my sister's body. "There's a cold spot inside her," he said. "It's cold and it's spreading. If we don't stop it, she'll die. We've got to heat her up from the inside. There's only one thing that will work." He went out, and a little while later he came back with some roots, each about the size of my little finger. He scraped off the skin and then sliced them up.

"I need a wooden bowl," he said. "We got to boil these."

In those days, when you wanted to offer a spiritual thing you used a wooden bowl, you didn't use the White Man's bowl.

"How you going to boil them in a wooden bowl?" my mother asked him.

Dr. Queen said, "You'll see."

So she gave him a wooden bowl with water in it. Dr. Queen put the roots in the bowl. Then he put it on a table and he held his hands over the bowl like you hold your hands over a hot stove. A whole crowd of people gathered around, watching him, wondering how he was going to make that water boil.

"Watch!" he said.

They watched. Pretty soon, someone said, "Look! Look!"

The roots started moving in the water, just a little at first, then more and more, until it seemed as if they were alive, wriggling around in the water like snakes.

And then they started to smoke!

There was no fire, mind you, just the wooden bowl sitting on the table. But the roots began to smoke. Pretty soon the water started boiling and steaming like water boils on a stove. But there was no stove.

"That's God's power," Dr. Queen told us.

Then he gave the bowl to my mother. "Strain it," he said, "then give it to her. Put it to her mouth with a wooden spoon."

So my mother gave the hot broth to my sister, who was still asleep. She put it to her lips with a wooden spoon and then let her sleep some more.

That night they held prayers for my sister at seven o'clock. They sang spirit-songs. I went back and forth from the prayer meeting to the tipi to see how my sister was doing. I thought she was going to die. So did everybody.

An hour later we were all standing around her. We were all crying. And then she opened her eyes. She sat up like she was waking from a nap. She yawned. She rubbed her eyes.

She looked at all of us.

"Why is everyone crying?" she asked.

Dr. Queen said, "Give her some more broth to drink." So my mother gave her some more broth and she drank it.

"Now let her rest," Dr. Queen said.

So after that we went back to the meeting and sang more spirit-songs. That happened about nine o'clock.

And all of a sudden, here she comes! My little sister, she came right up and stood beside me where we were singing. She was smiling. I asked her if she was all right.

"There's nothing wrong with me," she said. And there wasn't. She didn't even remember being sick.

So that's the power of God's medicine.

❖

# FINDING YOUR POWER

Every person has to find their own power, because each of us possesses a certain power. Search yourself for that power, know how to reach it inside yourself, and then use that power in harmony with God—for good and not for evil.

❖

# EVIL DEEDS

All our evil deeds are like dirty specks on a mirror. When we look for God we don't see Him clear because there are so many dirty specks. And He can't see us either.

❖

# LIES

Our word is sacred.

We never lie because God never lies.

It's the Law of Nature that you can't lie and get away with it. That's God's Law. You have to tell the truth.

If I do something wrong and you ask me about it, I say, "Yes, I made a mistake. I did it."

I wouldn't try to lie. I know God's listening.

If you lie, you've got to live with that lie all your life.

Nothing's heavier on your soul than a lie. Think of all the lies the White Man told the Indian. He made 371 treaties with us and he broke every one. All lies. That's a terrible burden on his soul. He thinks he got away with it. But he can't get away with it. God will make him pay.

God doesn't forget your lies.

And we Indians don't either.

❖

# A TALK WITH A CONGRESSMAN

I had a talk with a congressman about why we won't sell the Black Hills. He asked me, "King, why do you Indians need all that land? You don't do anything with the land you've already got. Why do you need more? We'll give you some money instead of those hills."

I told him, right there in the halls of Congress, with people all around listening, I told him:

"You say I don't *do* anything with my land? Well, what do you mean by doing? To the White Man, doing means changing things, destroying everything, chopping the forests and damming the rivers and polluting the skies. White Man wants us to be like him and build factories and motels and hamburger stands. We don't want those things!

"You say I don't *do* anything with our land? What I do is I live there by God's Law. That's what I do there."

I told that congressman, "I don't want to change or destroy it. It's my land. God gave me the title. You can't change that no matter how many lies you tell. No power on Earth can change that. Who do you think you are to tell me what to do on my own land? Only God tells me that!"

I started getting pretty mad. That was my wicked streak coming out again, you know.

Finally, I said to him louder than I should have, "You don't know what the hell you're talking about!"

Mathew King
*© 1994 by Chris Spotted Eagle*

I shouldn't have said that, I know. He's a congressman, a bigwig. People were standing right there listening. There were some ladies among them.

I told the ladies, "Excuse my language, but I feel like cussin'!"

Everyone laughed, except that congressman.

I thought I'd offended them. Instead, they applauded me—right there in the halls of Congress.

❖

# WHY I DO
# WHAT I DO

The other day I was thinking: Why am I doing all these things? Who gives me the direction?

Well, it comes from my mind, a kind of voice that says, "Mathew, you've got to do this!" So I get up and do it right away—because I know it's God who's giving me directions.

I know God is with me. I believe in God's power. We live by his power as we sit here and talk. That's God's power we're thinking with. It's God's mind. Our mind is part of God's mind. Our mind is part of Nature, part of God.

To Indians, Nature is God and God is Nature.

So when I work for my people, I'm working for God, I'm working for Nature.

Who are *you* working for?

❖

# WHAT YOU NEED TO DO

People ask me what they can do, what each of us can do. "Mr. King," they say, "how can we help Indian people? How can we make this a better world?"

I can't really tell them. It's got to come from them, not from me. I'm looking for their hearts. I'm trying to find their hearts. If I can touch them in their hearts, I know this will be a better world.

That's what I'm trying to do. Touch your heart. If I do that, then you'll know what to do.

❖

# About My Life

You should know who's telling you these things, so I'll tell you a little about my life.

I was born February 16, 1902, in Grass Creek, South Dakota, a little community of Indians from different bands. Our people settled there even before the massacre of Chief Big Foot and his people at Wounded Knee in 1890. The first thing they did was build a schoolhouse, then a church—an Episcopal church.

My mother, White Antelope, was Fast Thunder's daughter. My father, Yellow Shirt—Jefferson King—was Noble Red Man's son. He was quite a showman. He and my mother traveled with Buffalo Bill's Wild West show. When she wasn't traveling, my mother worked as a seamstress.

I was raised mostly by my grandparents. They gave me the proper training. They taught me about the Great Spirit and also the Christian God. I believed in both because I was taught both were the same.

You know, when White Man came here he sent the missionaries to conquer us. They wanted to convert the Indian people, but they were damn smart. They never converted all of us. That wasn't their aim. They always just converted some of us. Made some of us Christians while the others followed the traditional ways. That way they knew we would always fight among ourselves, so we could never be strong. That's how they tried to conquer us—and they're still at it today.

We lived very poor. In the early days we ate treaty food—the food the government gave us to fulfill the treaties. I remember those rations. The bacon was yellow and smelled bad. The rice and beans were full of mouse droppings. We picked out the droppings before we ate. We survived.

Grass Creek was a rough place to be a kid. There were lots of fights. I had to defend myself from an early age. I became a good fighter. My mother was always telling me it's wrong to fight, but I had no choice or I'd get beat up bad. It got so the bigger boys were afraid to fight me. They'd be the ones that wound up crying, not me. Finally they left me alone. So I survived all that, too.

Mrs. Hanson, an Englishwoman who taught at the Indian day school, told my mother I should try to learn the English language by going to the school, since my mother took me along every day when she worked there as a seamstress. My mother agreed, so I became a student at a very early age, only three-and-a-half years old.

It took me a long time to learn the English language. I couldn't make any sense of it at first. I only knew Lakota, so while I was trying to learn English I talked Lakota to Mrs. Hanson. One day she told my mother, "Mrs. King, I can't seem to teach English to Mathew, but he's doing a very good job teaching me Lakota!"

I became a good student, but I also acquired a bad habit. I started to smoke when I was four years old. I got that from my great-great-grandmother Cane Woman. She was in her nineties and she loved to smoke, but her hands shook so much she couldn't roll cigarettes. In those days people smoked Bull Durham tobacco. You rolled your own. Nobody wanted to roll all those cigarettes for Cane Woman, so she had me do it for her. That was hard for my little fingers at first, but after a while I mastered it. She'd always say, "Mathew, roll one and light me!" and I would put the cigarette in her mouth and light it. I tried a few puffs myself and I liked it. One day she said, "Roll one for yourself," which I did. I became a confirmed smoker after that.

Cane Woman was blind, and I had to guide her around with her cane. People really laughed when they saw us. She was the only woman who smoked, and I was the only little boy. We must have been quite a sight, the two of us, both smoking Bull Durham cigarettes while I led her around by the elbow.

Later, when they let me smoke the Peace Pipe at ceremonies, I was good at it right off. They told me the smoke carries our prayers right up to the Great Spirit, so I was grateful to Cane Woman for teaching me.

I became a cowboy at a very early age. I was the youngest cowboy, only six or seven years old. Both my grandfathers raised cattle and horses. I milked the cows every morning and evening. They would make me ride the calves of the milk cows, and when I got bucked off they'd laugh and laugh. I kept at it because I never got hurt, though later in my life I got hurt many times riding or breaking horses.

I can ride any wild horse that ever lived. I'm not afraid of them. I don't know why. I was wilder than any of them. I can speak to the horses.

© 1994 by Chris Spotted Eagle

Then my parents sent me off to high school, a military school. I stayed there four years. I was chief bugler. I had a colonel rating, but I wasn't commissioned. I could have been if I'd stayed there another year, but my parents wanted me to leave military school and go on to the seminary to study for the ministry. So that's what I did.

I'd had an early training in Christianity. My father and two uncles were converted by a missionary named Bishop Hare, who helped get us food in those early days when they took our guns and horses and we couldn't hunt anymore. If you converted you ate better. By then the buffalo were gone anyway. To help feed the starving Lakota my father and uncles became missionaries among their own people—ordained ministers in the Anglican Communion, or Episcopal Church. So, after high school, my mother sent me to a seminary to follow in their footsteps—the

Springfield Indian Seminary. I liked playing trumpet in the school orchestra, but I didn't want to become a minister.

I did a lot of serious thinking there at the Springfield Seminary. I came to the conclusion that what I was learning wasn't for me. It was White Man's Way, not Indian's Way. So I talked with the Bishop—Bishop Roberts. I asked him, "Bishop, can I do my missionary work in some other way than becoming a minister?"

He said, "What do you have in mind?"

I said, "You know, the Bible says you're supposed to earn your bread by the sweat of your brow. But right now a lot of our people don't know how to work—they don't know how to earn their bread by the sweat of their brow. So that's what I want to do instead of being a minister. I want to teach our people how to work so they can do what the Bible says and earn their bread by the sweat of their brow instead of going hungry."

"Good for you!" Bishop Roberts said. "I'll back you one hundred percent!"

And so I left the seminary. I looked for ways to put Indian people to work. The first year I took 250 Indians off the reservation to Sheridan, Wyoming, and Scotts Bluff, Nebraska. I got them work picking corn and sugar beets. Next year I took 500, the next 700, and finally I was getting work for 3,000 people—some Indians, some Mexicans, even whites. At first I was just a recruiter, then I worked as a field manager. After a while I was made supervisor. I taught a lot of Indians how to work, how to live in the White Man's world, how to survive by the sweat of their brow. I did that for many years.

I lived among the white people. I had many other jobs. I worked as a machinist in the aircraft industry. I worked for sugar companies.

I did construction work for the government. I always worked my way up to overseer or supervisor. Wherever I worked I always helped Indian people, helped get jobs for them, helped them survive.

Then, in 1940, I was made a headman, or subchief, by my people, the Oglala Lakota at Pine Ridge. In 1958 they made me a full chief. I became a spokesman for the chiefs. The seven bands of the Lakota elected me president. I was also elected president of the International Indian Treaty Council—so I became a spokesman for 280 tribes. At one time I was president of six different organizations. I made many trips to Washington to speak on behalf of our people. I traveled to France, England, Germany, Holland, South America, all over the world. I worked and lived for my people, to make their lives better.

Now I'm past eighty. I'm slowing down. I've retired from most things. These days I study the history of Indian religion. I'm trying to bring back all the things we lost. I teach the Sun Dance to Indians all over the country. I instruct the people how to do the sweat-lodge ceremony, how to nourish the roots of the sacred Sun Dance tree with our blood when we give God our flesh. I teach them how to talk to God. That's the best job of all.

So those are some of the things I've done with my life. It's been a hard life but a good life. I wouldn't want to live any other.

❖

# BEFORE THE WHITE MAN

No people on Earth ever enjoyed a freedom like we Indians enjoyed before the White Man came to this country. Everything was free. We were free and so were the animals and the birds and the rivers and the whole wonderful land from end to end. All free. All pure. All happy.

This was the freest and purest and happiest place in the whole Universe.

We were the Great Spirit's forest children, living free according to His Law.

Then Columbus and his gang hit this country by accident. We're sorry that they did.

Our Instructions didn't tell us what to do about the White Man. We welcomed him when he came here. We fed him. We took care of him. We believed God had sent him here to help us.

God gave the White Man powers we never saw before—material powers. He was supposed to share those powers to make life better for all of us. He was supposed to use the material power in the service of the spiritual power. He was supposed to connect them. He didn't. Instead, he used his material powers to steal our land and our freedom.

Now our great chieftains are gone. Our buffalo are gone. The country we loved is lost. They built roads over the fading trails where we once walked. Our weapons, our bows and arrows, our tomahawks are in the museums. They sell our arrowheads and even our bones for souvenirs. Maybe if we didn't remember how it once was it wouldn't be so bad for us. We could just become like everyone else.

Only one thing's sadder than remembering you once were free, and that's *forgetting* you once were free. That would be the saddest thing of all. That's one thing we Indians will never do.

❖

# A MESSAGE TO THE WHITE MAN

God put us both on this Earth, the Red Man and the White Man. I don't know why. There's a reason. I've looked for it all my life and I'm sorry to say I haven't found it. I can't understand why He sent you here to destroy His own Creation. It's a mystery. But God is always a mystery. I try to work with the mystery even when I don't understand it.

We're both God's children. When White
Man came here he said he was our Father. But
he's not. Only God is our Father, and the Earth
is our Mother. We Indians have proof of that,
because our skin is the color of Mother Earth.
God meant us to live in peace. He has a purpose
for each of us. He doesn't want one of us to kill
the other.

It's been a long war between our two
peoples. Five hundred years. We want it to end.
Maybe White Man thinks he's already won. But
you can't win when you go against God, against
Nature. All you win is God's wrath and God's
judgment.

God will always be the winner.

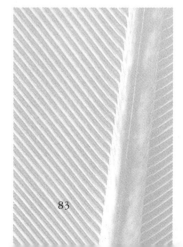

White Man has his own Way. He brought that Way here from across the ocean. He believes in it, though nothing good has come out of it that I can see. We don't believe in it. It's not our Way.

You've got your Holy Bible, and we've got our Sacred Pipe. Maybe God wants there to be both a Bible and a Pipe. We're not trying to convert you, and we don't want you to try to convert us. We only want our two peoples to live together in peace and mutual respect, each of us serving God in our way.

Isn't that acceptable to the White Man?

We don't condemn all white people. There are many good white people. They lead a good life. They don't do evil to others. They live with God. We don't hate anybody. Hating hurts the hater more than the one who's hated. We have no hate in our hearts. We hope there's none in yours. We open our hearts and our arms to you.

To tell you the truth, I don't know if we can ever really come together.

But I'm a dreamer, and I'll tell you my dream.

Someday Red Man and White Man will sit down with all the races of humankind and we'll solve our problems together. We'll all follow God's Law. We'll even pray together. You'll do it your way and we'll do it our way, but we'll all do it together.

Someday we'll have ceremonies together, and the eagle will come and join us. He'll dance with us. You'll learn what it's like to dance with the eagle.

It's true. We can all dance with the eagle. We can all fly with the eagle.

God would like that, I know. That's coming close. I'll be gone soon, so I probably won't see it, but maybe my grandchildren will see it—or their grandchildren.

Yes, it can happen. We'll all dance together with God!

❖

# REMEMBRANCES OF MATHEW

*WHILE GATHERING these materials, I had the opportunity to speak with some of Mathew's friends, family, and colleagues—people whose lives he shared and shaped. Here are some of their memories.*

*—Ed.*

JOE FLYING BY, a traditional Lakota elder from the Standing Rock reservation, recalls:

"Mathew King was a great man, a generous man. He gave his life to his people. He shared everything he had.

"He was a great chief, yes. But there are some chiefs who want to stand above the people. Mathew never tried to stand above the rest of us. It was always the people who pushed him up. That's why he was a great man.

"He was a singer, you know, a famous singer among our people. He taught us how to sing all the songs from long ago.

"The first time I got to know him was one summer at the Sun Dance at Green Grass, South Dakota, on the

Cheyenne River reservation, where they keep the Sacred Pipe. Mathew was the singer, but he was getting old and needed more singers. So he asked me, 'Please stay and help me. We need singers. I'll teach you the songs to sing.' So he taught me some new songs, songs he made up himself. I still sing them the way he taught me. Whenever we sing those songs today, Mathew's singing with us!

"Next day he took me aside. 'I know who you are,' he told me. 'You're a singer and you're going to be my son, my adopted son.' So I stayed there four days at the Sun Dance, and from that time on he was my father. He made me his adopted son. He was a father to all of us. He shared his songs like he shared his life and all that he had. He gave us everything. He gave us his heart.

"Yes, Mathew King was a great man."

DAVE CHIEF, a Lakota elder from the Pine Ridge reservation, remembers:

"When I was a boy, Mathew was already an Elder. Everyone knew him. He spoke for the people. He saved the old ways. He was always there when we needed him.

"Mathew could speak better than anyone else. He knew how to use words to make you understand. He was an explainer. He never lied. You always believed him.

"He was a Treaty Man. He never forgot the treaties we signed back in the old days. He worked all his life to get the Black Hills back. Every chance he got he talked about the Fort Laramie Treaty of 1868 and the other treaties.

"I remember, he used to come to meetings in a horse and wagon. He'd get up on the wagon and he'd call us all together and he'd stand there and tell us all about the treaties. He'd read them to us word for word. Then he'd explain what those words meant, one by one, and told us we were never to forget them. He wouldn't let us forget!"

❖

**CHARLES ABOUREZK**, a Rapid City lawyer deeply involved in Indian causes over the years, shares these memories of Mathew:

"Everyone looked up to Mathew. He was what Indians call 'a real Indian.' It's hard to put into words exactly what that means, because you have to be around for many years, watching that person in action, seeing them respond to every kind of situation, always putting the needs of the people before their personal needs. That was Mathew—a totally selfless man. He was one of the last of the older generation of Indians who had an absolute sense of being right, along with an unshakable sense of their own Indian identity. They looked on religion as something you live, not just a fixed set of beliefs. Mathew King was one of the most truly religious human beings I have ever known.

"You don't get the kind of reputation and respect he had among Indian people without earning it. He didn't care at all about material things, and you could tell that from the way he lived. He saw a lot of hard times. When he was a boy, he and his family used to go down to Nebraska to pick potatoes. He lived what Lakota people call *unshika*—or 'poor, humble.' But he was rich in everything that makes you a traditional Lakota leader and a respected Elder.

"He was a teacher as well as a leader. Whenever he'd see some young guys walking around stooped over, he'd go over and tell them loud and clear, 'Stand up straight! Put your shoulders back! Never forget—you're an Indian!' He taught young people how to walk right, not only literally but figuratively.

"Mathew was fearless. I remember, in 1981, I was with the Traditionals when they seized a piece of land in the Black Hills because the U.S. Forest Service had been routinely denying Indian applications for religious special-use permits. Mathew was more than just a spiritual advisor. He stepped right into the middle of it. He went in with us when we seized the site—we called it Yellow Thunder camp.

"We didn't know if the Feds would come in shooting or what. Mathew didn't show any fear. 'This is our land!' he kept saying, waving his cane in the air. 'The Black Hills are ours!' Some of the other guys were really scared, but Mathew's fearlessness was contagious. The way he talked gave them courage. He taught them fearlessness.

"He was the one who went to the Forest Service a couple of days later and signed the special-use application for 800 acres. Litigation went on for four years. Ultimately we lost the legal battle, but Yellow Thunder became a symbol of the struggle for the return of the Black Hills—which still goes on today.

"One interesting sidelight: When Mat signed the special-use permit application for Yellow Thunder camp, he didn't sign it 'Mathew King.' He signed it 'Noble Red Man.'"

❖

Yellow Thunder camp in the Black Hills

*© 1994 by Beyond Words Publishing, Inc., courtesy of Mathew King's family*

CHIEF OREN LYONS, Faithkeeper of the
Onondaga Nation and spokesman for the Six Nations
Iroquois Confederacy, shares these memories of Mathew:

"'*Washtay!*' was how he would greet us. That means
'Good!' in Lakota, and it was always good to see Mathew
King—Noble Red Man. Seeing him again would always
bring smiles to our faces, even in the gravest of emer-
gencies. Here was our great Lakota ally and friend,
joining us once more, bringing his special talents,
wisdom, and humor to our meetings.

"We, the Haudenosaunee (Six Nations Iroquois
Confederacy), met with the Lakota leaders many times
during the second fight at Wounded Knee in 1973. They
came to Onondaga during those times and we, the traditional Lakota and Haudenosaunee nations, struck a treaty
of peace and friendship and mutual support.

94

"Mat and Fools Crow made a formidable team that led the fight for the recognition of the Lakota treaties and the return of the Black Hills. They organized the Lakota Treaty Council, which was made up of traditional elders and leaders. I know Mathew would like to hear their names again, so I repeat some of them here: Kills Enemy, Iron Cloud, Bad Cob, Red Shirt, Bad Wound, Loud Hawk, Broken Nose, Star . . . . Those were all great names—and Noble Red Man was among them. They were patriots of the Great Sioux Nation. They were the old-style leaders—unselfish, compassionate, and always inspiring. They gave their time and their lives for their people.

"Mat was a leader among leaders. He directed much of the discussion as strategies were developed in the fight for the Black Hills against the might of the United States. We at Onondaga had a deep respect for those men and their families, because they understood and abided by the old honor system, which included humor as well as wisdom. They raised the hearts of the people just by their presence. Today we still honor that treaty between the Haudenosaunee and the Great Sioux Nation.

"Those were hard times for all of us, but hard times brought us together. Noble Red Man was a great part of that history.

"Mathew was a humorous man. You had to be alert when in his presence. That twinkle in his eye signaled some humorous trap that he could spring on you. He brought cheer into all of our hearts and lifted our spirits at the most difficult times. Even during life-and-death crises, our meetings were punctuated with loud roars of laughter—and more often than not it was Mathew who pointed out some ridiculous aspect of whatever was going on.

"That's what I remember best—his laughter, his inspiring laughter. He had a high-pitched voice, and his laughter made everyone else laugh. It made you feel good inside. His smile was as warm as sunlight and it shone on all of us."

❖

JOURNALIST KEVIN McKIERNAN, who was smuggled into Wounded Knee during the 1973 Occupation, shares this memory of the arrival of Frank Fools Crow and Mat King in the fortified compound at the height of the crisis:

"It was early in the Occupation, and the Feds let the two Elders, Frank and Mat, through the lines in hopes that they could convince the AIM 'hotheads' holding out inside to surrender. It was a really tense time, and the shooting could begin at any moment. The Feds had armored personnel carriers all around with machine guns mounted on top, and there were plenty of guns inside with the occupiers as well.

"Well, Frank and Mat came into the compound, and you never saw people so happy to see anyone. Frank said, 'They want us to intervene and stop the Occupation. That's why they let us through their lines, so we could convince you to surrender.'

"I remember, Frank was wearing one of those big black reservation hats the old-timers used to wear, the ones with the wide brims and tall crowns, big as cowboy hats.

"Mat said, 'They think we'll advise you to give up.' He had that twinkle in his eye that told you something was up.

"Then Frank spoke again, with Mat translating for those of us who didn't know Lakota.

"Frank said, 'You know, it's illegal for us to bring any supplies in here with us. It's a federal crime. They searched us before we came in. We know you people are hungry—you're suffering for all of us. And we want you to know we're with you one hundred percent!'

"He went on: 'They asked me to give them a sign how I'm voting, whether I want you to continue the Occupation or surrender. I wouldn't tell them how I'd vote, but I said I'd come in and talk to you, so they let us through.'

"Then Fools Crow said: 'And so I want to give you a sign about what to do. And this is the sign . . . .'

"With that, he raised his hand for silence, and then, with a sweeping gesture, he grabbed his big reservation hat by its wide brim and dramatically lifted it off his head. Everyone gasped, then they all laughed until they were rolling on the floor. Underneath Frank's hat, sitting right on top of his head, was a can of Maxwell House coffee!

"He and Mat had committed a federal crime—'aiding and abetting' the Occupiers by illegally transporting supplies to prolong what turned out to be the longest civil disorder in American history.

"I remember, Mathew had the shrillest laugh of all, a kind of tittering *hee-hee* that broke us all up again and again. His laughter was a kind of balm. It made us all feel good—full of hope, full of strength. He radiated a wonderful warmth that inspired everybody. He was a humble man without a shred of arrogance. When he talked to you, you felt like you were at the center of the universe. He and Frank were utterly different in their personalities, but both were spectacular human beings.

"So, anyway, that's how Maxwell House coffee became a kind of symbol of the Wounded Knee uprising!"

❖

LAVON KING, Mathew's daughter, recalls:

"I remember, when I was a child, Dad was always teaching us, always telling us what to do and what not to do. 'Be respectful of others,' he told us. 'Be honest and direct and don't ever lie. You can't fool the Great Spirit!'

"He got real mad whenever he read or heard that the Lakota people had been 'conquered.' 'Don't you ever believe that!' he taught us. 'They stole the land with their lies and greed and broken treaties, but they never conquered us in battle. We Lakota people have never been conquered and we never will be!'

"One thing for sure, they never conquered my Dad!

"Some of our young guys came to see him when he got ill, and they asked him, 'What are we going to do when you're gone and all the other Elders are gone?' He told them, 'Keep the Treaty going'—meaning the fight for the Black Hills. He said, 'Carry it on. Carry the Treaty. Carry the Pipe. Carry your people. You've got Lakota blood in your veins, don't you? As long as that blood flows through your veins you'll know what to do. You are the Elders now!'

"You know, most of their lives he and Chief Fools Crow worked together. Whenever the people needed them they were there, the two of them. Their lives were intertwined.

"When Dad passed away they brought Grandfather Fools Crow over. He stood there at the coffin just staring down a long time. He shook his head but he didn't say anything. Then he just turned around and they walked him out. Later, Grandma Nellie Red Owl went to see him, and she came back and told me, 'Fools Crow said that now that Mathew's gone, it's time for him to go, too. He said there was no one left he could share his dreams with anymore. He said there wasn't any reason for him to go on living—his work in this life was done.' Fools Crow died that same year. I know the two of them are together again now. They're watching over us.

"A few weeks back I climbed Bear Butte. I wanted to talk to my Dad. So much is going on these days, so

Bear Butte, sacred mountain of the Lakota
people in the Black Hills

© 1994 by Harvey Arden

many troubles, and there's no one like him around to talk to anymore. I wanted to ask him what I was supposed to do. So I went up on the mountain all by myself like he used to do.

"I prayed for a vision. Then I saw him. The sun was going down, and I could see him standing on the little peak across from the top of Bear Butte. He just stood there looking at me. I called out to him but he didn't answer. He had a stern look on his face, like he wasn't happy about something. I don't think he's mad at me. He knows I'm doing my best, just like he always taught me. I think it's the Black Hills he's mad about. He's still waiting for us to get them back. He won't rest until that happens—and neither will I!"

❖

SHARA GRIFFIN GONZALEZ, a friend of Mathew's, adds this memory:

"There was always something sweet and childlike about Mathew, despite his famous toughness. I remember, when he was sick near the end, I went to see him in the hospital. On his bedside table he'd arranged a whole menagerie of glass figurines. They were all animals—deer and rabbits and eagles and things like that. He told me he communicated with the spirits of the animals through the figurines, even though they were only glass.

"And then he told me, 'I'm sorry I don't have a bear. The bear is very important and I don't have one, so I can't talk to him. I wish I had a bear.'

"Well, of course, I went out and looked all over town for a glass figurine of a bear. I finally found one and brought it back to Mathew in the hospital. Oh, he was happy! It was the one he hadn't had, and now at last he had it. He smiled and smiled and talked to it like an old friend. 'That completes my collection!' he said. He thanked me again and again. So he had a special relationship to that little bear figurine.

"When he died, he was buried with it. I'll always be proud of that. It makes me feel closer to him."

❖

SCOTT BARTA, a Sun Dance singer, recollects Mathew's impact on his life:

"Whenever there was something going on about Indians, Mat and Fools Crow were there. You could always count on them. If they were around you knew the Great Spirit was nearby. I remember, when they came to the Crazy Horse Memorial at Fort Robinson, Nebraska, in 1977, Chief Fools Crow said the prayers and Mathew sang. Right then a big, dark cloud moved right over our heads and there was thunder and lightning. It was as if they'd called back the spirit of Crazy Horse himself. He always said he'd come back as thunder and lightning.

"Fools Crow would speak in Lakota and Mat would translate. No, more than just translate. He was Frank's official Interpreter. They knew each other so well, each of them knew exactly what the other was thinking. Sometimes someone would ask Frank a question and he'd just say a few words. Then Mathew would stand up and 'Interpret,' and his speech would go on for several minutes. You could see Frank nodding his head and grunting his approval. It was like they were thinking with the same mind.

"They were both leaders in reviving the Sun Dance. Back around 1974 or '75 they were at the Sun Dance in Green Grass, and my uncle—who later became Mat's adopted brother—asked Mat and Fools Crow if he had their permission to start the Sun Dance on the Yankton reservation. They told him, 'You don't need our permission. If it feels good, then do it. We'll help you. But only the Great Spirit gives permission!'

"That's the way they were, Mat and Frank—completely selfless people. I quit drinking because of those guys. So did lots of people. They had a tremendous influence, but they were two of the humblest guys you ever met. It's been a big loss, their passing. We could sure use 'em now. When you get to know men like that when you're young, you learn your own identity and it gives you strength, it leads you into the sweat lodge and into Lakota ways.

"But I remember Mat best as a singer. He knew the original Sun Dance songs from a million years ago, and he also composed wonderful new ones. One time we were singing with him at a Sun Dance and a big dragonfly— a *tusweyca*, we call it—came flying right into the ceremony. It had white and black stripes on its wings and it landed on the Sacred Tree. With every drumbeat its wings would flutter and whir, right in rhythm with the music. When we'd take a break, it would fly away. When we'd start again, it would return. All day it went on like that. Mat got really excited about it. 'It's come to sing with us two-leggeds,' he said. 'It's come to share our Sun Dance and pay respects with us to our Grandfather the Sun and our Grandmother the Earth. It's a messenger from the Great Mystery!' The tusweyca stayed with us all day until the sun went down. It was wonderful.

"There's a song I'd like to sing for you now. It's one of Mathew's songs. He composed it. He taught us every word, every intonation. I learned it from him and I sing it exactly as he taught it."

SCOTT SINGS *a poignant, soul-stirring melody in a rich tenor voice. When he finishes, I tell him: "I was crying while you sang that. It was like Mathew singing to me."*

*Scott explains:*

"It's a song they sing at the Sun Dance when you come into the arena, the Sun Dance circle. It's sung in the morning, when the sun comes up. They carry a buffalo skull into the Sun Dance circle and they sing it, Mathew's song. In English the words go something like this:

Friend, this is me.
Grandfather, I'm coming with the morning sun.
Hear me, I'm coming in.
This is me.
I greet you as you rise, Grandfather Sun.
I rise with you.
This is me.
Recognize me!

"Old Mathew—he really knew how to make the sun rise!"

❖

# EDITOR'S AFTERWORD

MATHEW KING passed away—or "took the Holy Road," as his people say—on March 18, 1989. Many times he spoke of his own impending death.

He once told me: "You know, last night I had a dream of my wife for the first time since she passed away four years ago. She came to me and she told me it's very peaceful up there. It's the best place, far from the wicked world. 'We lead a good life up here,' she said. She wanted me to hurry up and come on up there. So I told her, 'Wait a minute. I got a lot of things to do yet in the world. You better wait a little longer, then I'll be there.'"

Another time he said: "Now I'm old and I like to sleep late. I'm tired. I worked hard all my life, and it's time for me to rest. I'm going to die soon, I know it. I'm not worried about it. I've given everything I have to God. I know he's satisfied with me."

AFTER ONE of our conversations, Mathew had me set my pen on a chair cushion. He said he wanted to put a blessing on it—"so you don't do any harm with it to the Indian people."

He stood there before me, arms raised, and prayed

aloud for several minutes in the Lakota language. He talked to God, as he'd done so often throughout his life.

Then, finishing the prayer, he continued to stand there, head tilted back, eyes closed, listening. Listening to God. I could feel the spirit blowing right through us like a great wind.

Finally, he nodded, smiling that gentle smile of his, and said: "I told God what you're doing. He tells me you're going to have a good journey. No harm will come to the Indian people from what you're doing, and no harm will come to you while you're doing it."

I've done my best to live up to that over the years. I'll always be grateful for that blessing. It's carried me this far, and I suspect the journey isn't over. I'll still be needing it.

NOW THAT HE'S GONE ON to that "Great Reality" of which he spoke, the world is the poorer for his passing—but infinitely the richer for his having lived among us.

Mathew, thank you.

If Crazy Horse is to come back as thunder and lightning, I like to think that Mathew King—Chief Noble Red Man—will come back, too. Perhaps he'll come as rain, a gentle rain, pure and cleansing, falling on a spring day upon his beloved Black Hills. I know he'd like that.

❖

NATIVE AMERICAN BOOKS FROM
BEYOND WORDS PUBLISHING, INC.

WISDOMKEEPERS: Meetings with Native American Spiritual Elders
   *Authors: Harvey Arden and Steve Wall; Photographer: Steve Wall*
   *128 pages, $39.95 hardcover, $24.95 softcover, $16.95 audiotape*
   An extraordinary spirit-journey into the lives, minds, and natural-world philosophy of Native American spiritual Elders representing seventeen tribes. They are the Elders, the Old Ones, the fragile repositories of sacred ways and natural wisdom going back millennia. In the magnificent photographs and powerful words of the Wisdomkeepers, you share their innermost thoughts and feelings, their dreams and visions, their jokes and laughter, their healing remedies and apocalyptic prophecies. Above all, you share their humanity. Winner of four international design and printing awards. Printed on recycled paper with soy-based inks.

CEREMONY IN THE CIRCLE OF LIFE
   *Author: White Deer of Autumn; Illustrator: Daniel San Souci*
   *32 pages, $9.95 softcover*
   Little Turtle is an American Indian boy growing up in the city without knowledge of his ancestors' beliefs. He is visited by an Indian Spirit, who introduces him to his heritage and his relationship to all things in the Circle of Life.

NATIVE PEOPLE, NATIVE WAYS SERIES
   *Author: White Deer of Autumn; Illustrator: Shonto Begay*
   *88 pages, $5.95 softcover*
   The Native People, Native Ways series uses fiction and nonfiction to teach children about history through the eyes of North America's indigenous people. The four books in the series (*Book of Change, Book of Knowledge, Book of Life,* and *Book of Wisdom*) are designed around the Native American Circle of Life. The circle is divided into four sections, each representing one of the four directions of Man.

Beyond Words Publishing, Inc. • 1-800-284-9673